REDEEMED
from
SICKNESS

Receiving God's Promise of
Divine Health & Wholeness

T0026043

Bill Winston

Redeemed from Sickness: Receiving God's Promise of Divine Health and Wholeness

Copyright © 2023 by Bill Winston

Published by HigherLife Publishing & Marketing, Inc.
PO Box 623307
Oviedo, FL 32762
AHigherLife.com

Unless otherwise indicated, Scriptures are taken from the King James Version of the Bible.

Scripture quotations marked AMP are taken from the *Amplified Bible*. Copyright © 2015 by The Lockman Foundation. Used by permission. www.Lockman.org

Scripture quotations marked AMPC are taken from the *Amplified Bible, Classic Edition*. Copyright © 1954, 1958, 1962, 1964, 1965, 1987 by The Lockman Foundation. Used by permission. www.Lockman.org

Scripture quotations marked GNT are from the *Good News Translation in Today's English Version—Second Edition*. Copyright © 1992 by American Bible Society. Used by permission.

Scripture quotations marked NIV are taken from the *Holy Bible, New International Version®*, NIV®. Copyright © 1973, 1978, 1984,

Contents

Introduction

THERE IS NO MORE important subject in the Christian faith than the reality of redemption, which I am teaching in this book. Redemption goes way beyond your eternal salvation; it also covers every area of life here on earth before you get to heaven.

In *Redeemed from Sickness: Receiving God's Promise of Divine Health and Wholeness*, we will examine God's promises in the Bible for you to have a long, satisfying life, free from pain, sickness, and affliction, enabling you to receive wholeness in every area of your life.

"I pray that God, who gives peace, will make you completely holy. And may your spirit, soul, and body be kept healthy and faultless until our Lord Jesus Christ returns" (1 Thessalonians 5:23 CEV). Other translations say "wholly," meaning that your *whole* spirit, soul, and body will be kept sound and intact.

Let's start with the definition of *redeemed*, which means "to be brought or bought back." Sickness, disease, mental torment, and emotional distress hold multitudes of people captive today. As believers, we were in captivity, but we've been brought out of that captivity. Now we want to understand what it means to be brought out of death into life, sickness into health, bondage into freedom.

In *Redeemed from Sickness: Receiving God's Promise of Divine Health and Wholeness*, you will learn how to:

- Use your faith to walk in divine health and well-being.
- Activate the most powerful thing that exists.
- Access all the benefits Christ purchased for you.
- Possess your inheritance as a citizen of God's Kingdom.
- Experience the fullness of the gifts of the Holy Spirit.

God created you and placed you in the earth for such a time as this. It takes a healthy mind, heart, and body to fulfill the divine assignment that God has destined for you. As you read this book, begin today to walk in wholeness—spirit, soul, and body.

Faith Is the Foundation

Faith Dominates Time

As Christian believers we have dominion over the whole earth, which includes time. We are to take dominion over time. Faith is always now. Faith doesn't have to wait on time. When you lay hands on the sick and God heals them just like that, you just went around time. Time didn't hold you up.

Healing Has Become the Exception, Not the Rule

We have gotten away from some of the things that made the Church stand apart from the world, and one of them is divine healing. When somebody gets healed, it's looked at as an exception, like, "Whoa, they got healed!" instead of a confident expectation, like, "Yeah, she got healed."

I'm not saying that we minimize the work of God, because I know it's a supernatural work, but the point of it is that much of the time, if healing ever takes place, it's unexpected, as if God were doing a new thing! The truth is that healing is based on faith, and people have gotten away from faith. They have gotten away from believing, speaking, and acting on the word of faith. "But what saith it? The word is nigh thee, even in thy mouth, and in thy heart: that is, the word of faith, which we preach" (Romans 10:8).

Let's Go Up and Possess It

Do you remember when the children of Israel sent twelve leaders to spy out the land of Canaan? When they came back, ten of them gave an evil report. Only two, Joshua and Caleb, gave a good one.

Caleb said this: "Let us go up at once, and possess it" (Numbers 13:30). Notice, he was talking about a land that was populated with giants, a land in which the cities had walls around them that no man could penetrate. Yet he said, "Let us go up at once, and possess it." Did he know how they were going to conquer the land? No, but he was speaking the word of faith!

Recovering What's Been Lost

For the most part, the Church is not speaking the word of faith. *From this day forward, I'm declaring that we are bringing back the word of faith. We're recovering that which was lost.*

Caleb spoke something that to the natural mind sounded ridiculous and impossible. That's what faith does—it does the impossible! If you read Hebrews 11: "By faith Abel.... By faith Enoch.... By faith Noah.... By faith Abraham.... By faith.... By faith.... By faith...." All these seemingly impossible things were accomplished by faith.

Faith has nothing to do with your feelings. It is the act of believing the Word of God, speaking it, and expecting it to come to pass. That's the kind of faith that God has. When He saw darkness, He didn't say, "Ooh, isn't it dark out there?" He called darkness light—and light was!

Plant Your Faith Seed

The apostles asked the Lord to "increase our faith." How did Jesus respond? "And the Lord said, If ye had faith as a grain of mustard seed, ye might say unto this Sycamine tree, Be thou plucked up by the root, and be thou planted in the sea; and it should obey you" (Luke 17:5–6).

Over time, we began to deconstruct that particular verse, "Well, let's leave off the grain of mustard, and say it like this, 'If you had faith as a seed.'"

What do you do with a seed? You plant it. So, if you have faith as a seed, you'd speak out loud what you want it to do because when you say, you sow.

There's a Better Way

People have dealt with healing through many alternative methods. I'm talking about technology now. I'm talking about education. I'm talking about the hospitals, physicians, and specialists. Thank God for all of them, because if it weren't for them, some Christians would be dead.

But my point is that this was not the way God healed as He worked through the early Church. Jesus was their

Great Physician: "How God anointed Jesus of Nazareth with the Holy Ghost and with power: who went about doing good, and healing all that were oppressed of the devil; for God was with him" (Acts 10:38).

Don't feel condemned about what's in your medicine cabinet or about seeing doctors or going to the hospital. I'm not preaching against doctors or technology. I'm just telling you there is another way that doesn't include having a single scalpel cut your flesh. There is a way that won't include having to take a single dose of medication and deal with all the side effects that will come on you five years later. There is a way that doesn't include a single misdiagnosis. There is a way that doesn't include a single hospital bill. There is a better way!

It's Not God's Will for You to Be Sick

"He brought them forth also with silver and gold: and there was not one feeble person among their tribes" (Psalm 105:37). This is the account of the children of Israel coming out of the land of Egypt. They had been enslaved, beaten, and mistreated for four hundred years. They were poor, but God delivered them, brought justice, and recompensed them for all that they'd suffered.

Not one feeble person was among their tribes. God never intended for His children to tolerate any sickness at all. How many did it say were feeble when they came out? Not one! Out of three million people, not one of them was sick or weak!

Are There Any Sick among You?

In James, we read instructions about this to the believers in the church. When people were sick, their first thought was not to head to the ER, but to call for the church leaders to pray for them.

> **Are there any sick among you? Then ask the elders of the church to come and pray over the sick and anoint them with oil in the name of our Lord. And the prayer of faith will heal the sick and the Lord will raise them up, and if they have committed sins they will be forgiven.**
>
> —James 5:14–15 TPT

Sometimes, people feel like they don't deserve to be healed. "You don't know what I've done," they say. It doesn't matter. God is full of mercy and is ready to heal you if you're ready to receive. Get rid of the guilt—it's not from God!

What is your first thought when sickness or affliction attacks your body? As I said before, I'm not coming against doctors or medicine, but what I want to point out here is about image.

Your Image Dictates Your Future

The children of Israel came out of Egypt, but Egypt hadn't come out of them. When Moses had gone up on the mountain to receive the Ten Commandments and stayed there for forty days, the Israelites decided to make a golden calf as their god. Now, where'd the calf come from? It came from the image placed in them by the Egyptians because two of their many gods were a calf and a bull.

If the image that's been placed in you is that the doctor at the hospital is your healer, then when pressure comes, that's where you'll go. And that's fine, but as I mentioned before, there's a better way.

Your Healer Is Jehovah

Your healer is Jehovah! He said, "I am Jehovah Rapha! I am the God that heals you!" Even if God uses a surgeon, a nurse, or other medical professional, the Healer is still God. *The Expanded Bible* says,

> If you worship the LORD your God, I [he]
> will bless your bread and your water. I will
> take away sickness from you. None of your
> women will miscarry or be unable to have
> children [barren]. I will allow you to live
> long lives [fill the number of your days].
>
> —Exodus 23:25-26 EXB

Not only did the Lord promise no sickness, but He also said none of the women would be barren (a source of shame for women of that day), and every one of them would live a long, healthy life. No early or premature deaths!

I Am

In Exodus 15, God introduced Himself as the Healer:

> He said, "If you listen carefully to the LORD
> your God and do what is right in his eyes,
> if you pay attention to his commands and

**keep all his decrees, I will not bring on
you any of the diseases I brought on the
Egyptians, for I am the LORD, who heals
you."**

—Exodus 15:26 NIV

The King James Version says, "I will put none of
these diseases upon thee." And that word *put* really should be in the permissive: "I will [permit] none
of these diseases upon thee, which I have [permitted
to come] upon the Egyptians: for I am the Lord that
healeth thee."

A Hebrew translation says, "I am thy Great
Physician."

CHAPTER 2

Forget Not All His Benefits

NO SICKNESS OR DISEASE was tolerated in Israel. This well-known psalm, praising the Lord for all His many benefits, is recorded in the Bible as being written by King David:

> Bless the LORD, O my soul: and all that
> is within me, bless his holy name. Bless
> the LORD, O my soul, and forget not
> all his benefits: who forgiveth all thine
> iniquities; who healeth all thy diseases; who
> redeemeth thy life from destruction; who
> crowneth thee with lovingkindness and
> tender mercies; who satisfieth thy mouth
> with good things; so that thy youth is
> renewed like the eagle's.
>
> —Psalm 103:1–5

It doesn't matter what disease you've been diagnosed with or what guilt or trouble you're experiencing; it's got to go! God's Word promises forgiveness, vibrant health, freedom from destruction, good things, youthfulness, and all that His lovingkindness and mercy can bring. Praise the Lord!

Delivered from Destruction

"He sent his word, and healed them, and delivered them from their destructions. Oh that men would praise the LORD for his goodness, and for his wonderful works to the children of men!" (Psalm 107:20-21).

He didn't send the Word, and *sometimes* it healed them. No, "He sent his word, and healed them," which tells me that sickness (and the root of sickness) is spiritual. That's why you can curse cancer or any other disease at the root, and it has to obey you!

The Physician Who Never Lost a Patient

I know this teaching is powerful, and I'm certainly not talking against our physicians, who have studied hard and earned medical degrees. Thank God for them, but

I tell you something greater: there is a Physician who has never lost a patient.

The world doesn't know anything about this, so they need to go to a doctor and get medical help. But if you're born again, you are a citizen of God's Kingdom, and you can operate supernaturally according to His ways.

Consider this: gauge yourself, because if you're not ready to receive your healing by faith and you have to go to the doctor, that's fine. Go to the doctor and use your faith when you're at the doctor's office because if you go to the hospital, you're sure enough going to need to use your faith there.

When you take medication, take it by faith in Jesus' Name. Say, "I take this in Jesus' Name. Lord, take all the impurities out of this medication, all the side effects. I believe I am divinely protected from anything that is harmful, in the Name of Jesus. Amen!"

She Was Desperate to Get Her Healing

Remember the woman with the issue of blood? The Bible said she had gone to all the physicians, but she was not better; she rather grew worse. Here's the story in Mark 5:

> And a certain woman, which had an issue of blood twelve years, and had suffered many things of many physicians, and had spent all that she had, and was nothing bettered, but rather grew worse, when she had heard of Jesus, came in the press behind, and touched his garment. For she said, If I may touch but his clothes, I shall be whole. And straightway the fountain of her blood was dried up; and she felt in her body that she was healed of that plague.

> And Jesus, immediately knowing in himself that virtue had gone out of him, turned him about in the press, and said, Who touched my clothes?

> And his disciples said unto him, Thou seest the multitude thronging thee, and sayest thou, Who touched me?

> And he looked round about to see her that had done this thing. But the woman fearing

**and trembling, knowing what was done in
her, came and fell down before him, and
told him all the truth. And he said unto her,
Daughter, thy faith hath made thee whole;
go in peace, and be whole of thy plague.**

—Mark 5:25–34

This woman had a continual issue of blood for twelve years! She said, "If I may touch but his clothes, I shall be whole," so she touched Jesus' garment. She pressed her way through a crowd. Now, let me show you what's wrong with what she did.

Quarantined!

Under Old Testament law, a woman with an issue of blood was unclean and had to be separated from everybody for a period of time.

**And if a woman have an issue, and her issue
in her flesh be blood, she shall be put apart
seven days: and whosoever toucheth her
shall be unclean until the even. And every
thing that she lieth upon in her separation
shall be unclean: every thing also that she
sitteth upon shall be unclean.... Every
bed whereon she lieth all the days of her**

issue shall be unto her as the bed of her separation: and whatsoever she sitteth upon shall be unclean, as the uncleanness of her separation. And whosoever toucheth those things shall be unclean, and shall wash his clothes, and bathe himself in water, and be unclean until the even.

—Leviticus 15:19–20, 26–27

Faith Overrides the Law

Here's this woman with the issue of blood, and the Law said she had to be separated for seven days. If that issue of blood didn't stop, then she was going to be unclean and anything she touched was going to be unclean, including her husband. And she had this problem for twelve years! This woman was in a place where she couldn't even have relationships, but then she heard about Jesus!

She said, "Now, if I can just touch His clothes." Well, what's wrong with that? She knew the Law, but see, once you come into faith, it overrides the Law!

She touched His clothes and immediately felt in her body that she was healed of that plague. Jesus looked around to see who touched Him, and His disciples didn't even catch it. They said, "Lord, all these people are pushing on You. Everyone is touching You. What do You mean?"

But Jesus said, "No, no, somebody touched Me." See, up until that time she was a nobody, but that all changed because when you touch Jesus, you become a somebody!

Instantly She Was Healed

Understand, when God does something, it doesn't take all day. We're not talking about a treatment here; we're talking about divine healing.

God can do it right away. I want you to get that in your spirit. I know we can take some medication and work with it over six months, but we're not talking about that. We're talking about straightening you up right now. The woman was healed instantly, and she didn't have to spend a dime for it!

CHAPTER 3

The Most Powerful Thing That Exists

S AY THIS WITH ME: "All disease is from the devil." See, you've got to be firm in that because you can't get healed saying God is putting this disease or that disease on you. God doesn't cause any disease.

Say this with me: "The Word of God is the most powerful thing that exists." There are some powerful things in the natural world. How about the atomic bomb? That's pretty powerful, isn't it? The Word of God is more powerful! How about a storm—a tornado or a hurricane? No man has invented anything to stop a hurricane.

Can the Word stop a storm? Yes! Jesus told a storm, "Peace, be still," and the thing stopped immediately.

Just think of any disease that might have come into your body. Well, the Word of God is more powerful than that disease—it's the most powerful thing that exists. Its purpose is to destroy the works of the devil. Remember, your focus isn't on the disease; it's on the Word of God.

Natural Things Must Obey the Spoken Word of God

Have you ever thought, "If only I had more faith"? The apostles did. They wanted to know how they could get more faith. "And the apostles said unto the Lord, Increase our faith" (Luke 17:5).

Jesus replied to the apostles' request for more faith, "If ye had faith as a grain of mustard seed, ye might say unto this Sycamine tree, Be thou plucked up by the root, and be thou planted in the sea; and it should obey you" (Luke 17:6). If you're a believer in Jesus and speak according to His Word, nothing can escape your faith command.

Faith and the Word are synonymous. You can't have the Word without faith, and you can't have faith without the Word. Got it? Once you get the Word, you've got faith.

In verse 6, the word *might* in the original Greek actually means "would"— we can really say, "Ye would say unto this Sycamine tree." Now, a Sycamine tree is a big tree that has berries on it that we call mulberries, and it's not really a fit source of food. It's something undesirable.

You've Got to Get to the Root

Jesus said we might say to this Sycamine tree, "Be thou plucked up by the root." Remember this: Everything that you can see has something behind it that you can't see. *Everything physical was first spiritual.*

"Be thou plucked up by the root, and be thou planted in the sea; and it should obey you." Whom should it obey? You!

You don't deal with the problem; you release faith, which is a servant of the believer. Faith goes out and starts to go to work not on the leaves but *on the root*. It goes all the way down to the source of your sickness and will root it out!

Your Faith Does the Work

You don't work faith; you come to a rest. Faith does the work. Jesus spoke once to a fig tree, left, finished His business, and returned the way He'd come (Matthew 21:19). What was faith doing while He slept? Working!

Jesus didn't say, "I'm going to get this tree out of the way. Bring Me that Mini Mac chainsaw. Bring me that ax over there." He went back to how Adam dealt with things in the Garden. Jesus just spoke to them because He learned that from His Daddy.

Are You Willing to Be Laughed At?

The same story is seen in Mark 11. Jesus is hungry and looks for fruit on the tree. There is none, so "Jesus answered and said unto it, No man eat fruit of thee hereafter for ever. And his disciples heard it" (Mark 11:14).

Suppose you see me speaking to a tree on the side of the road as you're passing by in a car. What would you think? When you step out in the God-kind of faith, it could look a little ridiculous, but you must be willing to take the ridicule.

When I was believing God to buy a shopping mall, I went down to the barbershop. Lesson learned: when you're believing God for something don't go down to the barbershop or the beauty salon. Don't go by there. Get your hair done in your kitchen.

So, at the barbershop they told me, "Reverend, I hear you're going to get that mall," and then they winked at each other.

I answered them, "Well, yeah."

"What are you going to do with that?" they asked.

And I repeated, "Yeah, we're going to get it." I was a little bit timid back then about saying what I should've said. I wasn't going to get it; I believed I already had it!

But I didn't say that, and when you don't speak faith, you're diluting your faith and contaminating it with fear. Folks, we're coming to a place now where we're going to have to take Jesus public. He's either going to be your Lord, or you'll deny Him like Peter did!

Have the God Kind of Faith

Jesus was willing to take the ridicule, but when they came back the following day the tree was dried up, and they called it to His attention. They said, "Master, behold, this thing You spoke to, this thing is dried up from the roots." What did Jesus say? "Well, have faith in God, or have the God kind of faith." (See Mark 11:20–22.)

This God kind of faith moves mountains:

> **For verily I say unto you, That whosoever shall say unto this mountain, Be thou removed, and be thou cast into the sea; and shall not doubt in his heart, but shall believe that those things which he saith shall come to pass; he shall have whatsoever he saith. Therefore I say unto you, What things soever ye desire, when ye pray, believe that ye receive them, and ye shall have them.**
>
> —Mark 11:23–24

Notice, you have to *speak* and *believe* for the promise to manifest. Don't let the devil talk you out of the point between "when you believe you receive" and "there it is!" You've got to stay with it, and hold fast the confession of your faith without wavering for He who promised is faithful to do it!

Faith Works by Love

Another thing about this God kind of faith is that it works by love. This is shown in the very next verse:

"And when ye stand praying, forgive, if ye have ought against any: that your Father also which is in heaven may forgive you your trespasses" (Mark 11:25).

Did somebody do you wrong? You're going to have to forgive them to walk in the God kind of faith, which was what the Father and Son demonstrated: "But God commendeth his love toward us, in that, while we were yet sinners, Christ died for us" (Romans 5:8).

If God, through the death of His Son, forgave us our sins, how much more should we forgive those who have hurt us? Holding unforgiveness in your heart can block your healing and the answers to your prayers because it hinders your faith: "Faith ... worketh by love" (Galatians 5:6).

Find the Promise for Your Faith to Stand On

The faith of God was given to you when you got born again. If you want to use that faith, you've got to get a promise for that faith to stand on. In other words, faith for the promise is in the promise itself.

If you want to get faith for healing, you need to get some promises on healing because "faith cometh by hearing, and hearing by the word of God" (Romans 10:17). Then, faith comes in and fills up your heart, and "out of the fullness (the overflow, the superabundance) of the heart the mouth speaks" (Matthew 12:34 AMPC). Once you release the promise out of your mouth, it has divine energy that is more powerful than anything that exists!

The Spirit Was in Him

"And Jesus returned in the power of the Spirit into Galilee: and there went out a fame of him through all the region round about. And he taught in their synagogues, being glorified of all" (Luke 4:14–15).

Jesus enters a synagogue on the Sabbath and stands up to read:

> The Spirit of the Lord is upon me, because he hath anointed me to preach the gospel to the poor; he hath sent me to heal the brokenhearted, to preach deliverance to the captives, and recovering of sight to the blind, to set at liberty them that are bruised, to preach the acceptable year of the Lord.

> And he closed the book, and he gave
> it again to the minister, and sat down.
> And the eyes of all them that were in the
> synagogue were fastened on him. And he
> began to say unto them, This day is this
> scripture fulfilled in your ears.
>
> —Luke 4:18–21

In other words, He declared, "*I'm* the fulfillment of this scripture." What was the response of the people in the synagogue? Instead of believing, they became enraged at Him.

Unbelief Stops Mighty Works

While faith is the most powerful thing that exists, it can be stopped cold. How? Through unbelief! Mark 6 shows how even Jesus "could there do no mighty work" in His own hometown because of their unbelief.

> And he went out from thence, and came
> into his own country; and his disciples
> follow him. And when the sabbath day was
> come, he began to teach in the synagogue:
> and many hearing him were astonished,
> saying, From whence hath this man these
> things? and what wisdom is this which

> **is given unto him, that even such mighty
> works are wrought by his hands? Is not this
> the carpenter, the son of Mary, the brother
> of James, and Joses, and of Juda, and
> Simon? and are not his sisters here with us?
> And they were offended at him.**
>
> —Mark 6:1–3

Notice they're trying to discredit His ministry. Who does He think He is?

> **But Jesus said unto them, A prophet is not
> without honour, but in his own country,
> and among his own kin, and in his own
> house. And he could there do no mighty
> work, save that he laid his hands upon a few
> sick folk, and healed them.**
>
> —Mark 6:4–5

In other words, the Bible says, "save that he laid his hands upon a few sick folk, and healed them," meaning people with minor ailments like a headache. Jesus, the Miracle Worker, could do no mighty works!? Why? The answer is in verse 6: "And he marveled because of their *unbelief*. And he went round about the villages, teaching" (emphasis added).

Where Is Your Trust?

See, when you don't see God as your Source and you don't see Him as your Healer, as far as He's concerned, you're in unbelief. You can go to the doctor and the doctor can work with you, but who do you place your trust in? Your trust should be in God, not the physician.

It's the same with a job. Somebody says, "Well, I'm going to live by faith and quit my job." But, if you can't live by faith with a job, how are you going to quit your job and live by faith? Living by faith doesn't mean you quit your job; it means you don't see the job as your source.

You can go to the hospital, and you can go to the doctor; just don't see them as your source. They aren't the source. That's why God's raising up Holy Ghost doctors. A Holy Ghost doctor can listen to God, and God will tell him, "See, right here is the problem."

Unbalanced Teaching

Don't be ashamed or afraid of what some people may think or say, "Well, I don't know. I feel condemned going to the doctor. I don't want any of the church folks to see me." There's been some unbalanced teaching on this. If you go to the hospital or take medication, that doesn't mean you're in unbelief.

Do what you need to do. When you get full of faith and you're fully persuaded, you won't even have to deal with it. You won't have to be struggling, "I wonder: Should I go or not?" No, it won't even cross your mind.

God Finds Faith Outside of His People

Back at the synagogue in His hometown, Jesus was not accepted because of their lack of faith. He began to talk about a woman of Zarephath, to whom God sent the prophet Elijah. (See 1 Kings 17.) God commanded her to take care of Elijah. Why? Because there was unbelief in Israel. Nobody in Israel would receive Elijah or what he said. He could speak the word of faith, and they wouldn't even believe it. If you don't believe it, you can't receive it!

Though this woman was not a part of the tribes of Israel and was outside the covenant, she believed the covenant and later received a miracle from God.

Another time God's mercy reached outside His own people was in the story of Naaman, a Syrian army leader, who had leprosy. Second Kings 5 tells the story:

> **And the Syrians had gone out by
> companies, and had brought away captive
> out of the land of Israel a little maid; and
> she waited on Naaman's wife. And she said
> unto her mistress, Would God my lord were
> with the prophet that is in Samaria! for he
> would recover him of his leprosy.**
>
> —2 Kings 5:2–3

There Is a Prophet in Israel

One of Naaman's servants told him about the prophet in Israel that could cure his leprosy. Naaman, being a great leader, headed out to see the king of Israel, bringing with him many riches as a gift. The king sent him to Elisha. "So Naaman came with his horses and with his chariot, and stood at the door of the house of Elisha" (verse 9). Watch what happened next:

> **And Elisha sent a messenger unto him,
> saying, Go and wash in Jordan seven times,
> and thy flesh shall come again to thee,
> and thou shalt be clean. But Naaman was
> wroth, and went away, and said, Behold, I
> thought, He will surely come out to me, and
> stand, and call on the name of the LORD**

his God, and strike his hand over the place, and recover the leper. Are not Abana and Pharpar, rivers of Damascus, better than all the waters of Israel? may I not wash in them, and be clean? So he turned and went away in a rage.

—2 Kings 5:10–12

He said, "Ah," took his horse, turned around, and rode away. Now what caused that reaction? Pride.

Pride Will Keep You from Your Blessing

What happened then? His servant was running alongside him and said, "Master, wait a minute. If the prophet would've told you to do something great, wouldn't you have done that?" Naaman thought about it and said, "Well, yeah, I think I would."

Naaman wisely set aside his pride and obeyed the instructions given him by Elisha's servant: "Then went he down, and dipped himself seven times in Jordan, according to the saying of the man of God: and his flesh came again like unto the flesh of a little child, and he was clean" (2 Kings 5:14).

If this woman of Zarephath and this army captain from Syria—neither of them part of God's covenant with Israel or the Church—could believe and receive, how much more can we born-again believers today believe and receive our healing or miracle from God?

Notice one important thing in both of these stories: they didn't just believe; they also *acted* on the instruction they were given. Faith without works is dead. Take heed to the instruction in the story about Jesus at the wedding of Cana in John 2 where Jesus' mother said, "Whatsoever he saith unto you, do it" (John 2:5).

My friend, whatever you are seeking from God today—healing, a financial or family miracle, or freedom from addiction—whatever Jesus tells you, just do it!

CHAPTER 4

Healing Is Now

Most Christians agree that we've been redeemed from sin through the blood of Jesus Christ, but remember that we've also been redeemed from sickness and the curse that was placed on the earth after Adam's transgression in the Garden.

We can still live in the earth, but we can be separate from the world and the calamity in it. He has set us apart from the things that come on the world that we call curses. We are redeemed from the curse of the Law.

> **Christ hath redeemed us from the curse of the law, being made a curse for us: for it is written, Cursed is every one that hangeth on a tree: that the blessing of Abraham might come on the Gentiles through Jesus**

> **Christ; that** *we might receive the promise of*
> *the Spirit through faith.*
> —Galatians 3:13–14 emphasis added

Notice, these things are not automatic. Scripture says we "receive the promise of the Spirit through faith" (Galatians 3:14), so we're going to have to apply faith to make this happen.

What Is Faith, and How Do We Get It?

What is faith? "Now faith is the substance of things hoped for, the evidence of things not seen" (Hebrews 11:1).

The Amplified Bible says it this way:

> **Now faith is the assurance (title deed, confirmation) of things hoped for (divinely guaranteed), and the evidence of things not seen [the conviction of their reality— faith comprehends as fact what cannot be experienced by the physical senses].**

This verse tells me that something (substance) is there, and even though you can't see it with the natural eye, *it is still there.* How do we get it? We get it by faith, which comes only one way:

So then faith cometh by hearing, and hearing by the word of God.

—Romans 10:17

That means if something isn't happening in somebody's life, it's because either they've heard it and not acted on it or they've never heard it at all. If you've been on the road to Mississippi for forty years and haven't gotten there yet, either you're on the wrong road or your car is not working. I mean there is something wrong here.

The Spirit of God Lives in You

Let's look at some places where the enemy perhaps has painted some defective pictures in our minds of what God says in His Word. The devil comes to steal, kill, and destroy, and has distorted God's truth, so we want to erase some lies and build a sure foundation in our lives.

God does not want us to be ignorant about the things of the Spirit. Remember, we read in Galatians 3:14 that He gives us the promise of the Spirit by faith. Fifty days after Jesus ascended to the Father, the Spirit first came to live within the believers. (See Acts 2.)

This is the fruit of the Spirit living in us that should flow out toward others: "But the Holy Spirit produces this kind of fruit in our lives: love, joy, peace, patience, kindness, goodness, faithfulness, gentleness, and self-control. There is no law against these things!" (Galatians 5:22–23 NLT).

The Holy Spirit Imparts Spiritual Gifts

First Corinthians 12 describes the spiritual gifts that are sovereignly distributed to God's people (the Church) for the benefit of all.

> Now concerning spiritual gifts, brethren,
> I would not have you ignorant.... Now
> there are diversities of gifts, but the
> same Spirit. And there are differences of
> administrations, but the same Lord. And
> there are diversities of operations, but it
> is the same God which worketh all in all.
> But the manifestation of the Spirit is given
> to every man to profit withal. For to one is
> given by the Spirit the word of wisdom; to
> another the word of knowledge by the same
> Spirit; to another faith by the same Spirit;
> to another the gifts of healing by the same

Spirit; to another the working of miracles; to another prophecy; to another discerning of spirits; to another divers kinds of tongues; to another the interpretation of tongues: but all these worketh that one and the selfsame Spirit, dividing to every man severally as he will.

—1 Corinthians 12:1, 4–11

Holy Spirit Gifts Are for the Body of Christ

In other words, the Holy Spirit comes and divides these gifts among the people in the Body of Christ or the local church as He wills. You and I don't know when He will manifest a spiritual gift or through whom He will manifest it. The only thing we know is that these Holy Spirit gifts are given to the Body of Christ and could come on my life or your life.

Let's examine a couple of the gifts. Verse 9 says, "to another faith by the same Spirit." God can give you an impartation of faith so that you can receive or do certain things. Verse 9 continues, "to another the gifts of healing by the same Spirit." Somebody could have a gift placed on them by the Holy Spirit so that they can actually pray for people who, let's say, have cancer and every one of them gets healed. Or they can pray for people who have arthritis and every one of them gets healed. Glory to God!

Walking as Mere Men

In 1 Corinthians 3:1, we see that Paul is talking to people who are immature and still carnal, walking in strife, envy, and division. He calls them "babes in Christ," and the *Amplified Bible* says they are "mere infants." This means you're still walking around as natural men. You're not able to operate in the things of faith. The best thing He can do for you is give you gifts because you can't operate via the faith route.

See, with a gift of faith I don't know when the gift is coming. That gift might be here tomorrow or it might not be here until next year. I'm just waiting.

There's Something Better

Thank God for spiritual gifts, but there is something better. When I say something better, I mean that God intended for you to operate in what you have already.

If I'm mature, then instead of waiting on the gift of faith, I have faith because of my hearing, believing, and receiving the Word of God. That Word changes my believing on the inside, and I'm ready to speak and act on what I believe. I don't have to wait for the Holy Spirit to sovereignly place a spiritual gift on me. Instead, when I speak and act on what I believe, it will happen as I release my faith.

When you're working your faith, you can work it *now*. When you're waiting on the gifts, you have to wait until the Spirit wills. You can receive now from Jesus, whether it's healing, family reconciliation, or finances like in this story in Matthew.

Supernatural Provision

Jesus provided money supernaturally to take care of His and Peter's tax debt. Let's pick up the story in Matthew 17:

> **And when they were come to Capernaum,**
> **they that received tribute *money* came to**
> **Peter, and said, Doth not your master pay**
> **tribute?**

> He saith, Yes. And when he was come into
> the house, Jesus prevented him, saying,
> What thinkest thou, Simon? of whom
> do the kings of the earth take custom
> or tribute? of their own children, or of
> strangers?
>
> Peter saith unto him, Of strangers. Jesus
> saith unto him, Then are the children free.
>
> —Matthew 17:24–26

This means they were tax exempt! Praise God!

> Notwithstanding, lest we should offend
> them, go thou to the sea, and cast an hook,
> and take up the fish that first cometh up;
> and when thou hast opened his mouth,
> thou shalt find a piece of money: that take,
> and give unto them for me and thee.
>
> —Matthew 17:27

Now, when was the tax money due? It was due now!
And when did Jesus receive the money? Now!

You Can Be Healed Now!

This same supernatural provision can be applied to
your healing. How?

Our minds have to be renewed. When we come into the Kingdom, we've got to understand the fact that if we are in God, we're in eternity, which means there is no time. You and I have been taught to live and think time. Almost everything we relate to and speak about, we speak according to time. Your flesh has been trained for time, and your mind has been programmed for time: tomorrow, next week, payday is coming Thursday, and so on.

Once you get into the Kingdom and understand your dominion over time, you can understand that payday is when you say it is! Isn't that what Jesus said to Peter when He told him to go fish for the money to pay their taxes? You don't need to wait on your next payday to get some tax (or any other) money!

"But, beloved,"—that's you He's talking to—"be not ignorant of this one thing, that one day is with the Lord as a thousand years, and a thousand years as one day" (2 Peter 3:8).

It doesn't make any difference whether you're talking about a thousand years or one day because it's all the same to God. Eternity doesn't have time. God's time is always now.

Jesus Operated in This Kind of Faith

Jesus operated in this kind of faith and manifested it any time He needed it. For example, when He was going to feed five thousand men plus women and children, He needed two fish and five loaves of bread. When did He need it? Now! When did He multiply it? Now! Jesus operated in faith that always produced at the time it was needed—a NOW kind of faith!

I'm saying this because as a man thinketh in his heart so is he. (See Proverbs 3:27.) If your thinking is limited to time, you can't operate out of time. You've got to renew and reprogram your mind that there is no time. By faith, you've got to believe that, and reinforce it by speaking in agreement with God's Word.

Jesus Was Wounded for You to Be Healed

Look at this often-quoted "healing" scripture in 1 Peter 2, and note the word I have emphasized: "Who his own self bare our sins in his own body on the tree, that we, being dead to sins, should live unto righteousness: by whose stripes ye *were* healed" (1 Peter 2:24 emphasis added).

Does this verse say you're going to be healed some-time in the future? No! It says healing has already tak-en place. Let's look at a couple of related scriptures.

> **Surely He has borne our griefs (sicknesses, weaknesses, and distresses) and carried our sorrows *and* pains [of punishment], yet we [ignorantly] considered Him stricken, smitten, and afflicted by God [as if with leprosy]. But He was wounded for our transgressions, He was bruised for our guilt *and* iniquities; the chastisement [needful to obtain] peace *and* well-being for us was upon Him, and with the stripes [that wounded] Him we are healed *and* made whole.**
>
> Isaiah 53:4–5 AMPC emphasis added

Notice that in these verses in which the prophet is looking forward to the cross, it says you *are* healed. That's when He took your sicknesses and pains, so you don't have to be sick!

Jesus Fulfills the Prophecy

This scripture also refers back to the prophecy by Isa-iah quoted in Matthew:

> **That evening many people with demons in them were brought to Jesus. And with only a word he forced out the evil spirits and healed everyone who was sick. So God's promise came true, just as the prophet Isaiah had said, "He healed our diseases and made us well."**
>
> —Matthew 8:16–17 CEV

God's promises are for you today. There is no future in God; there is only right now. When you agree with God, you've got to say it like God says it: "With Jesus' stripes I am healed!" The Word of God is stronger than any sickness or problem you might be facing. It can put limbs back together; it can take a person who is out of their mind and put them in their right mind.

Whom the Son Sets Free Is Free Indeed

I pray for you right now, my friend. Whatever sin, sickness, or affliction you are experiencing has already been nailed to the cross. You are forgiven and delivered from every addiction and demonic attack. You are healed and made whole with the stripes of Jesus Christ, in Jesus' Name. Amen!

CHAPTER 5

Confession Is the Cornerstone of Christianity

W E LIVE IN A time-controlled world, and many times we are going to have to say something that doesn't seem reasonable to the people around us. It's calling things that are not as though they were. We have to get accustomed to "talking out of time in time," and often it is saying something that people's minds are not going to agree with or understand.

We have to say what the Bible says when the world says just the opposite. Realize, you're not trying to lift yourself up; what you're doing is putting a spiritual law in motion—the law of confession.

You Have to Confess It Before You Can Possess It

Confession is the cornerstone of Christianity. And what you confess, you can possess. For example, take this Scripture: "That if thou shalt confess with thy mouth the Lord Jesus, and shalt believe in thine heart that God hath raised him from the dead, thou shalt be saved" (Romans 10:9).

You're going to have to confess that Jesus is your Lord and that you are in Him before you get in Him, before you are saved. Now that you're born again in Him, you're going to have to say what God says to activate God's blessings and promises in your life.

It may not seem reasonable, but that's only because we've been programmed by a system that was designed to keep us from receiving our inheritance, which includes healing, prosperity, protection, and all the benefits of the Kingdom of God.

Here's the proof: God saw a world that was dark, void, and formless, and He said one thing: "Let there be light." His word rearranged the earth! God loaded that same faith He used to create the world into His Word and gave that Word to you. Same faith! It'll change and rearrange your community. You've got to believe what you say is going to come to pass, and you will see it. (See Mark 11.)

Words Govern the Earth

"Death and life are in the power of the tongue" (Proverbs 18:21). In Genesis 1, God gave man instructions to govern the earth: "And God blessed them, and God said unto them, Be fruitful, and multiply, and replenish the earth, and subdue it: and have dominion" (Genesis 1:28).

Do you think money governs this earth? No, words govern this earth. Do you think money determines how much is in your wallet or bank account? No, words determine this too. Start agreeing with God's Word: "But my God shall supply all your need according to his riches in glory by Christ Jesus" (Philippians 4:19).

Are you feeling weak in your body, or inadequate to accomplish a task? Agree with Philippians 4:13: "I can do all things through Christ which strengtheneth me."

Understand this: words control it all. If I want to get somewhere, I've got to change my words. Start saying the same thing that God says, and you'll end up where you want to be in life. It doesn't matter how the situation looks!

No Worldly System Can Hold You Captive

It doesn't matter what system put you there! A man can be in prison and be innocent of that crime. He can speak right words and get out. There's no system on earth that can overcome the words you believe and speak when they agree with God's Word!

This is a revelation for the Body of Christ. Why? Because God has called us to rule and reign, and He is backing His words and working through us.

You are not the overlord of your life. You need a higher power, and there are only two choices: one is God, and the other is the devil. Both of them are vying for the authority that you have on the earth. The war is in the mind. The enemy tries to shoot thoughts into your mind to make you say words that are crosswise to God's Word. Or he'll put a pain or sickness in your body.

Now, you've got a choice! You can go with your flesh, "Aw, Lord, I'm sick!" Or, you can confess, "I've been healed by the stripes of Jesus." The word *confession* in the New Testament comes from the Greek word *homologeo*, which means "agreement." Do you agree with God?

Scripture Is Given to Perfect the People of God

The Word of God is given to you and me to equip, correct, and instruct us to live out our Kingdom destiny on the earth: "All scripture is given by inspiration of God, and is profitable for doctrine, for reproof, for correction, for instruction in righteousness: that the man of God may be perfect, thoroughly furnished unto all good works" (2 Timothy 3:16–17).

All Scripture is given by inspiration of God. Doctrine is instruction, and reproof is conviction. I can give you a word, and it has the power to convict you. Correction removes error from your thinking and your life. Instruction in righteousness is training in righteousness.

Saying the Wrong Thing Brings Wrong Results

One example in the Bible of how saying the wrong thing brought disastrous results is the story of Job. Remember how the devil stole everything Job had, including his health, his children, and his property? How did it happen? First of all, Job was filled with fear that his children had sinned and evil would come to them. "For the thing which I greatly feared is come upon me, and that which I was afraid of is come unto me" (Job 3:25).

We are in a war, and fear is your enemy! Fear is faith in what the devil can do to you. It is the opposite of the God kind of faith. We are admonished to "fight the good fight of faith" in 1 Timothy 6:12.

Secondly, Job not only feared in his heart, but he spoke words of fear. Exactly what he spoke came to pass. We need to learn a lesson here to put our trust in God and not fear what the devil can do because he was defeated at the cross. All we have to do is enforce that defeat with our words of faith and victory!

Later on, Job learned that lesson as he asked of God, "Deliver me from the enemy's hand? or, Redeem me from the hand of the mighty? Teach me, and *I will hold my tongue*: and cause me to understand wherein I have erred" (Job 6:23–24 emphasis added). Sometimes it's best not to say anything at all rather than saying something that doesn't agree with God's Word.

Words Can Pull Down the Hedge of God's Protection

Words are controlling this planet. The devil knows it. He's trying to keep you separated from the revelation and understanding of the power of your words. Satan put that thought in Job's mind, and consequently, Job spoke something. When Job spoke, he pulled down the hedge of God's protection. You may say, "Well, God allowed it." God will allow exactly what you will allow.

Fear isn't the only thing that can open the door to demonic attack. Sometimes, when we get hit with sickness, an unexpected financial debt, a family crisis, or whatever it might be, we ask, "How did that happen?" Our natural minds cannot comprehend how we allowed the devil to get in and attack us. What we need is God's wisdom.

Ask for God's Wisdom in Your Situation

The Book of James has a lot to say about the tongue and wisdom. For now, let's focus on how we get wisdom that will help us in whatever situation we're facing.

> My brethren, count it all joy when ye fall
> into divers temptations; knowing this, that
> the trying of your faith worketh patience.
> But let patience have her perfect work,
> that ye may be perfect and entire, wanting
> nothing. If any of you lack wisdom, let
> him ask of God, that giveth to all men
> liberally, and upbraideth not; and it shall
> be given him. But let him ask in faith,
> nothing wavering. For he that wavereth is
> like a wave of the sea driven with the wind
> and tossed. For let not that man think that
> he shall receive any thing of the Lord. A
> double minded man is unstable in all his
> ways.
>
> —James 1:2–8

Now, satan is coming in and tempting me. A trial has come into my life. If any of you lack wisdom as to how that trial got into your life, let him ask God. He will give you wisdom liberally if your faith does not waver. Say this with me: **"I receive wisdom from God for [name a situation for which you need wisdom]."**

CHAPTER 6

Possessing Your Inheritance

I N CHAPTER THREE OF this book, we talked about how "the blessing of Abraham might come on the Gentiles through Jesus Christ; that we might receive the promise of the Spirit through faith" (Galatians 3:14). The Blessing wasn't only for Abraham and his natural descendants—it belongs to you and me too because "Christ hath redeemed us from the curse of the law, being made a curse for us" (Galatians 3:13).

To see all that's in this blessing and included in your inheritance, read Deuteronomy 28:1–14. Read the rest of that chapter to see all that we've been delivered from next. Praise God!

We can learn what God has for us by what He promised to give Israel as their possession:

> When the LORD thy God shall bring thee
> into the land whither thou goest to possess
> it, and hath cast out many nations before
> thee, the Hittites, and the Girgashites,
> and the Amorites, and the Canaanites,
> and the Perizzites, and the Hivites, and
> the Jebusites, seven nations greater and
> mightier than thou... .
>
> —Deuteronomy 7:1

Note that God tells His people, "These nations are greater than you. These nations are mightier than you." God is telling you right now that what He's taking you in to face is bigger than you are. It's mightier than you are. It might be richer than you or have more influence than you too, but it doesn't make any difference because it's coming down. If it's a part of your promise, your inheritance, God's going to bring it into your hands.

The Battle Is the Lord's

Verse 2 of Deuteronomy 7 continues: "And when the Lord thy God shall deliver them before thee; thou shalt smite them, and utterly destroy them; thou shalt make no covenant with them, nor shew mercy unto them."

Whatever our enemy is—sickness, lack, strife—we are to show no mercy and make no covenant (agreement) with it. It's His battle; God shall deliver us from the enemy.

He's going to be with us. He's got to be the One who goes with us to make this happen. We cannot do it in our own strength.

The description continues in Deuteronomy 9:

> **Hear, O Israel: Thou art to pass over Jordan this day, to go in to possess nations greater and mightier than thyself, cities great and fenced up to heaven, a people great and tall, the children of the Anakims, whom thou knowest, and of whom thou hast heard say, Who can stand before the children of Anak! Understand therefore this day, that the LORD thy God is he which goeth over before thee; as a consuming fire he shall destroy them, and he shall bring them down before thy face: so shalt thou drive them out, and destroy them quickly, as the LORD hath said unto thee.**
>
> —Deuteronomy 9:1–3

Possess Your Promised Land

These mighty people, the children of Anak, had quite a reputation. Notice that God tells the Israelites to go and possess this land. This is not only a command of God but a responsibility. We have to possess our own promised land. The Promised Land in that time was the land of Canaan. The promised land for us is the promises that God has outlined in His Word.

Note that He says that in that day, there were giants in the land. There were enemies occupying the land. It's the same thing now. Satan is still trying to keep us from possessing God's promises—our inheritance.

The Enemies Are Driven Out and Destroyed

The Book of Joshua is the book of faith, and it's also a war book in the Old Testament that chronicles the time period in which the people of God were going in to possess the inheritance God had for them. God told them to destroy the enemy, but look what happened:

> **As for the Jebusites the inhabitants of Jerusalem, the children of Judah could not drive them out: but the Jebusites dwell with**

> **the children of Judah at Jerusalem unto this day.**
>
> —Joshua 15:63

> **And they drave not out the Canaanites that dwelt in Gezer: but the Canaanites dwell among the Ephraimites unto this day, and serve under tribute.**
>
> —Joshua 16:10

To "serve under tribute" means they lived as slaves, but they still lived with them.

> **Yet the children of Manasseh could not drive out the inhabitants of those cities; but the Canaanites would dwell in that land. Yet it came to pass, when the children of Israel were waxen strong, that they put the Canaanites to tribute; but did not utterly drive them out.**
>
> —Joshua 17:12–13

The Israelites forced the captives to work as slaves but did not completely drive them out. In each one of these cases, the Israelites didn't drive them out. In other words, they somewhat occupied the land that God said He'd given as an inheritance to His people.

> **And there remained among the children
> of Israel seven tribes, which had not yet
> received their inheritance. And Joshua said
> unto the children of Israel,** *How long are
> ye slack to go to possess the land,* **which the
> LORD God of your fathers hath given you?**
> —Joshua 18:2–3 emphasis added

"How long are ye slack?" That's a question that could be asked of us as a Church or as individuals. How long are you going to be slack in going in and possessing what God has promised you? As a seed of Abraham these promises are yours.

God Has More for You than Salvation

Being born again is the starting point, but it's not all there is. God wants you to experience deliverance. He wants you to experience joy. He wants you to experience victory. God wants you to experience health, and He wants you to experience wealth. All these Kingdom blessings are yours.

See, you got born again, and you can thank God for that, but don't let the devil sit on your healing. Jesus bore your sicknesses, weaknesses, and pain in His body on the cross. The work's been done. Just receive it!

What If I've Sinned?

Here's what the Bible says about your sin: "This is the covenant that I will make with them after those days, saith the Lord, I will put my laws into their hearts, and in their minds will I write them; and their sins and iniquities will I remember no more" (Hebrews 10:16–17). Now that's for you.

If you're born again, you're under the blood of Jesus Christ and you're forgiven. First John 1:9 gives us instructions on how to get rid of that sin: "If we confess our sins, he is faithful and just to forgive us our sins, and to cleanse us from all unrighteousness."

The devil tries to bring up our past, but all we have to do is repent and confess our sins according to 1 John 1:9. It also says this in Isaiah 43:25: "And yet, I am the God who forgives your sins, and I do this because of who I am. I will not hold your sins against you" (GNT). The King James Version and most other English translations say that He "will not remember" your sins.

God will forgive us and forget our sins. So now, after our confession of sin, we can say, "I have never done wrong."

The word *forgiveness* in the Greek has to do with purging or cleansing. Sin is expunged from His records and expunged from your life. God now sees you through the blood of His dear Son and treats you like you never did anything wrong.

CHAPTER 7

Raising the Dead

There's nothing too hard for God. Jesus paid the price for it all—every sickness, every addiction, every demonic attack. Not even death can resist the power of God to heal, deliver, and restore life. In this chapter, I want to look at three instances when the dead were raised.

First, let's look at the story of the ruler's daughter who was very sick—so sick she died as her father was imploring Jesus to come heal his daughter.

> **While he spake these things unto them, behold, there came a certain ruler, and worshipped him, saying, My daughter is even now dead: but come and lay thy hand upon her, and she shall live. And Jesus arose, and followed him, and so did his disciples.... And when Jesus came into the**

> **ruler's house, and saw the minstrels and the people making a noise, he said unto them, Give place: for the maid is not dead, but sleepeth. And they laughed him to scorn. But when the people were put forth, he went in, and took her by the hand, and the maid arose. And the fame hereof went abroad into all that land.**
>
> **—Matthew 9:18–19, 23–26**

When Jesus walked into Jairus' house, Jairus' daughter was dead. All the evidence that she was dead was there: she wasn't breathing; they were weeping and wailing and planning a funeral. Yet Jesus walked in and said, "She's not dead; she's just asleep." Though humanly speaking, it looked like the young girl had died, Jesus' word overcame even death.

His Word Was with Power and Authority

"And [Jesus] came down to Capernaum, a city of Galilee, and taught them on the sabbath days. And they were astonished at his doctrine: for his word was with power" (Luke 4:31–32). Did you know that even in

God's house, there are people possessed with devils? Continuing in verse 33, we read about such a case in Jesus' day:

> **And in the synagogue there was a man, which had a spirit of an unclean devil, and cried out with a loud voice, saying, Let us alone; what have we to do with thee, thou Jesus of Nazareth? art thou come to destroy us? I know thee who thou art; the Holy One of God. And Jesus rebuked him, saying, Hold thy peace, and come out of him. And when the devil had thrown him in the midst, he came out of him, and hurt him not. And they were all amazed, and spake among themselves, saying,** *What a word is this!* **for** *with authority and power* **he commandeth the unclean spirits, and they come out.**
>
> —Luke 4:33–36 emphasis added

When you begin to operate according to how Jesus operated, you're going to have some problems with religious people. Why couldn't these people believe? They weren't heathen; they were religious people faithfully attending the synagogue. Hebrews 4:2 gives the answer: "For unto us was the gospel preached, as well as unto them: but the word preached did not profit them, not being mixed with faith in them that heard it."

You'll find the same thing in some churches today: "These people honor me with their lips, but their hearts are far from me. They worship me in vain; their teachings are merely human rules" (Matthew 15:8–9 NIV). No power, just tradition or watered-down teachings!

The Promise Is Already Yours

There is nowhere in the Bible that says you're going to be healed. If you say, "I'm going to be healed" (in future tense), then you're not in faith. And, if you're not in faith, God is not bound to deliver you because you can only receive His promises through faith.

Faith is always *now*. I *am* healed with the stripes of Jesus—not I'm going to be. Your healing occurred two thousand years ago when Jesus paid the price for you to be healed. When will your healing take place? "What things soever ye desire, *when ye pray*, believe that ye receive them, and ye shall have them" (Mark 11:24 emphasis added). When? Now!

"All Is Well"

How about the Shunammite woman who took care of the prophet Elisha whenever he passed through her town, even setting up a room for him? Because she was so kind to him, Elisha prophesied that she would have a son at a certain time, and she gave birth.

When the son grew to be about twelve years of age, he went out with his father in the field. The son became ill and died, so his mother laid him on the bed in Elisha's room. Let's pick up the story there:

> And she called unto her husband, and said,
> Send me, I pray thee, one of the young
> men, and one of the asses, that I may run
> to the man of God, and come again. And
> he said, Wherefore wilt thou go to him to
> day? it is neither new moon, nor sabbath.
> And she said, It shall be well.… So she went
> and came unto the man of God to mount
> Carmel. And it came to pass, when the
> man of God saw her afar off, that he said to
> Gehazi his servant, Behold, yonder is that

> **Shunammite: run now, I pray thee, to meet her, and say unto her, Is it well with thee? is it well with thy husband? is it well with the child?** *And she answered, It is well.*
> —2 Kings 4:22–23, 25–26 emphasis added

Elisha sent his servant, Gehazi, ahead with Elisha's own staff to lay it upon the boy to raise him from the dead. Gehazi obeyed but couldn't raise the boy to life. So Elisha followed the Shunammite to where her dead son lay.

> **And when Elisha was come into the house, behold, the child was dead, and laid upon his bed. He went in therefore, and shut the door upon them twain, and prayed unto the LORD. And he went up, and lay upon the child, and put his mouth upon his mouth, and his eyes upon his eyes, and his hands upon his hands: and stretched himself upon the child; and the flesh of the child waxed warm. Then he returned, and walked in the house to and fro; and went up, and stretched himself upon him: and the child sneezed seven times, and the child opened his eyes. And he called Gehazi, and said, Call this Shunammite. So he called her.**

**And when she was come in unto him, he
said, Take up thy son.**

—2 Kings 4:32–36

So the man of God said, "Aye, uh, how is it with you? Is it well with you? Is it well with your husband? Is it well with your son?" Guess what she said, "All is well. All is well." Folks, if that doesn't qualify for a lie, I don't know what does.

But how can you lie saying what God said? You can't! If He says that by His stripes you are healed, then you're healed! This lady wasn't looking at the circumstances; she was speaking the desired outcome by faith —and it came to pass just as she said!

Greater Works than Jesus

The Bible says Jesus always spoke the words of God, and that's why God gave Him the Spirit without measure. He gave Him the power without limit. In the same way, Jesus gives us the power to heal and set the captives free. *The Passion Translation* says this: "I tell you this timeless truth: The person who follows me in faith, believing in me, will do the same mighty miracles that I do—even greater miracles than these because I go to be with my Father!" (John 14:12).

Loose Him and Let Him Go

Do you remember the story of Lazarus, Jesus' friend, whom he loved? Let's pick it up in John 11:

> Now a certain man was sick, named
> Lazarus, of Bethany, the town of Mary and
> her sister Martha. (It was that Mary which
> anointed the Lord with ointment, and
> wiped his feet with her hair, whose brother
> Lazarus was sick.) Therefore his sisters sent
> unto him, saying, Lord, behold, he whom
> thou lovest is sick.
>
> –John 11:1–3

You would think Jesus would rush to the scene to help his friends, wouldn't you? But this is what actually happened:

This Sickness Is Not unto Death

> When Jesus heard that, he said, This
> sickness is not unto death, but for the
> glory of God, that the Son of God might be

> glorified thereby. Now Jesus loved Martha,
> and her sister, and Lazarus. When he had
> heard therefore that he was sick, he abode
> two days still in the same place where he
> was.
>
> —John 11:4–6

Jesus went on to explain to His disciples that they would go back to Judea despite their reminders to Him that this was where people had tried to stone Him.

> These things said he: and after that he saith
> unto them, Our friend Lazarus sleepeth;
> but I go, that I may awake him out of sleep.
> Then said his disciples, Lord, if he sleep,
> he shall do well. Howbeit Jesus spake of his
> death: but they thought that he had spoken
> of taking of rest in sleep. Then said Jesus
> unto them plainly, Lazarus is dead. And I
> am glad for your sakes that I was not there,
> to the intent ye may believe; nevertheless let
> us go unto him.
>
> —John 11:11–15

"Whatever You Ask, God Will Give You"

So, Jesus and His disciples started on the journey. "Then when Jesus came, he found that he had lain in the grave four days already" (John 11:17).

> Then Martha, as soon as she heard that Jesus was coming, went and met him: but Mary sat still in the house. Then said Martha unto Jesus, Lord, if thou hadst been here, my brother had not died. But I know, that even now, whatsoever thou wilt ask of God, God will give it thee. Jesus saith unto her, Thy brother shall rise again. Martha saith unto him, I know that he shall rise again in the resurrection at the last day.
>
> —John 11:20–24

Jesus Says, "I Am the Resurrection!"

> Jesus said unto her, I am the resurrection, and the life: he that believeth in me, though he were dead, yet shall he live: and whosoever liveth and believeth in me shall never die. Believest thou this? She saith

unto him, Yea, Lord: I believe that thou art
the Christ, the Son of God, which should
come into the world.

—John 11:25–27

Martha went on her way. Mary came out to see Jesus and said basically the same thing as her sister. The mourners followed, and some of them questioned why Jesus allowed Lazarus to die. Jesus went to the gravesite: "Jesus therefore again groaning in himself cometh to the grave. It was a cave, and a stone lay upon it" (John 11:38).

Believe and You Will See the Glory of God

Jesus said, Take ye away the stone. Martha,
the sister of him that was dead, saith unto
him, Lord, by this time he stinketh: for
he hath been dead four days. Jesus saith
unto her, Said I not unto thee, that, if thou
wouldest believe, thou shouldest see the
glory of God? Then they took away the
stone from the place where the dead was
laid. And Jesus lifted up his eyes, and said,
Father, I thank thee that thou hast heard

**me. And I knew that thou hearest me
always: but because of the people which
stand by I said *it*, that they may believe
that thou hast sent me. And when he thus
had spoken, he cried with a loud voice,
Lazarus, come forth. And he that was dead
came forth, bound hand and foot with
graveclothes: and his face was bound about
with a napkin. Jesus saith unto them, Loose
him, and let him go.**

—John 11:39–44

Not only physical death, but whatever is "dead" in your life—your health, your finances, your relationships, your dreams and goals—can be resurrected just like the Shunammite's son, the ruler's daughter, and Lazarus by the Word of God and the touch of the Master.

Jesus said, "The thief comes only in order to steal, kill, and destroy. I have come in order that you might have life—life in all its fullness" (John 10:10 GNT).

Conclusion

"I S ANY SICK AMONG you?" is the question asked in the Bible (James 5:14). That would be a strange question to ask in today's society because the answer would be, "Yes, of course! Many are sick." Mankind has made much progress in the fields of medicine and science and developed cures for many diseases that plagued past generations. Yet many are still sick, depressed, and without hope.

In the Church it should be different. As I've pointed out in this book, the Church's mandate—yours and mine—is to establish the Kingdom of God on the earth. God's ways are higher; they are supernatural and not subject to the natural limitations of man.

As believers in Jesus, we are to be operating in divine health and prosperity in every area of our lives. His blood was shed not only for our eternal salvation but also for the healing of our souls and bodies. "Beloved, I wish above all things that thou mayest prosper and be in health, even as thy soul prospereth" (3 John 2).

God wants everybody healed, and He can heal everybody because He healed them in the Old Testament. Look at how Jesus' ministry fulfilled the prophecy that was quoted earlier in Isaiah 53:4–5:

> **That evening many people with demons in them were brought to Jesus. And with only a word he forced out the evil spirits and healed everyone who was sick. So God's promise came true, just as the prophet Isaiah had said, "He healed our diseases and made us well."**
>
> —Matthew 8:16–17 CEV

You might say, "Yeah, but that was Jesus. I'm not a teacher or minister; I'm just a normal person." If you have Christ living in you, you are not just a normal person—*you* have His power and authority over sickness and demons. (See Luke 9.)

The Great Commission, including healing, was passed on to the disciples in the early Church, "Great numbers of people swarmed into Jerusalem from the nearby villages. They brought with them the sick and those troubled by demons—and everyone was healed!" (Acts 5:16 TPT).

Healing didn't pass away after the early Church. The commission to preach the Kingdom of God and heal the sick is still ours today. How much more now should we be walking in divine health when we have all of His gifts and spiritual weapons given to us through the Holy Spirit?

Prayer for Salvation

Heavenly Father, I come to You in the Name of Your Son, Jesus Christ. You said in Your Word that whosoever shall call upon the Name of the Lord shall be saved (Romans 10:13). Father, I am calling on Jesus right now. I believe He died on the cross for my sins, was raised from the dead on the third day, and is alive right now. Lord Jesus, I am asking You now, come into my heart. Live Your life in me and through me. I repent of my sins and surrender myself totally and completely to You. Heavenly Father, by faith I now confess Jesus Christ as my new Lord and Savior and from this day forward, I dedicate my life to serving Him.

Prayer for the Baptism of the Holy Spirit

My Heavenly Father, I am Your child, for I believe in my heart that Jesus has been raised from the dead and I have confessed Him as my Lord. Jesus said, "How much more shall your heavenly Father give the Holy Spirit to them that ask Him" (Luke 11:13). I ask You now in the Name of Jesus to fill me with the Holy Spirit. I step into the fullness and power that I desire in the Name of Jesus. I confess that I am a Spirit-filled Christian. As I yield my vocal organs, I expect to speak in tongues as the Spirit gives me utterance in the Name of Jesus. Praise the Lord! Amen.

Scripture References

- John 14:16–17
- Luke 11:13
- Acts 1:8
- Acts 2:4
- Acts 2:32–33, 38–39
- Acts 8:12–17
- Acts 10:44–46
- Acts 19:2, 5–6
- 1 Corinthians 14:2–15
- 1 Corinthians 14:18, 27
- Ephesians 6:18
- Jude 20

William (Bill) Samuel Winston

B ILL WINSTON IS THE visionary founder and senior pastor of **Living Word Christian Center** in Forest Park, Illinois.

He is also founder and president of **Bill Winston Ministries**, a partnership-based global outreach ministry that shares the gospel through television, radio, and the internet; the nationally accredited **Joseph Business School** which has partnership locations on five continents and an online program; the **Living Word School of Ministry and Missions**; and **Faith Ministries Alliance (FMA)**, an organization of more than 800 churches and ministries under his spiritual covering in the United States and other countries.

The ministry owns and operates two shopping malls, **Forest Park Plaza** in Forest Park and **Washington Plaza** in Tuskegee, Alabama.

Bill is married to Veronica and is the father of three, Melody, Allegra, and David, and the grandfather of eight.

Books by Bill Winston

- *Be My Witness: Demonstrating the Spirit, Power, and Love of God*
- *Born Again and Spirit-Filled*
- *Climbing without Compromise*
- *Divine Favor — Gift from God, Expanded Edition*
- *Faith and the Marketplace: Becoming the Person of Influence God Intended You to Be, Revised and Expanded Edition*
- *Faith in the Blessing*
- *Imitate God and Get Results*
- *Possessing Your Mountain*
- *Power of the Tongue*
- *Revelation of Royalty: Rediscovering Your Royal Identity in Christ*
- *Seeding for the Billion Flow*
- *Supernatural Wealth Transfer: Restoring the Earth to Its Rightful Owners*
- *Tapping the Wisdom of God*
- *The God Kind of Faith, Expanded Edition*

- *The Kingdom of God in You: Releasing the Kingdom, Replenishing the Earth, Revised and Updated*
- *The Law of Confession: Revolutionize Your Life and Rewrite Your Future with the Power of Words*
- *The Missing Link of Meditation*
- *The Power of Grace*
- *The Power of the Tithe*
- *The Spirit of Leadership: Leadership Lessons Learned from the Life of Joseph*
- *Training for Reigning: Releasing the Power of Your Potential*
- *Transform Your Thinking, Transform Your Life: Radically Change Your Thoughts, Your World, and Your Destiny*
- *Vengeance of the Lord: The Justice System of God*

Some books are available in other languages.

Connect with Us!

Connect with Bill Winston Ministries on social media.

Visit www.billwinston.org/social to connect with all of our official social media channels.

Bill Winston Ministries

P.O. Box 947

Oak Park, Illinois 60303-0947

(708) 697-5100

(800) 711-9327

www.billwinston.org

Bill Winston Ministries Africa

22 Salisbury Road

Morningside, Durban, KWA Zulu Natal 4001

+27(0)313032541

orders@billwinston.org.za www.billwinston.org.za

Bill Winston Ministries Canada

P.O. Box 2900 Vancouver BC V6B 0L4

(844) 298-2900

www.billwinston.ca

Prayer Call Center

(877) 543-9443